Sew Simple Hexi-
Karin Hellaby

Quilters Haven
Publications

About the author

Karin Hellaby is the owner of Quilters Haven in Suffolk, a quilt shop and online business. She is a graduate textiles teacher who enjoys travelling and teaching classes all over the world.

As well as writing books, Karin blogs and has contributed articles to UK magazines. She has appeared on the Quilt Show and QNNTV, and has her own YouTube channel.

Karin is the quilting expert adviser for Arena Travel UK, a specialist tour company that arranges holidays for quilters in Europe, North America and Asia.

Karin feels her greatest achievement has been to bring up three sons on her own.

She started writing books to support them through university. All three are working in London and the eldest, Ross, is soon to take up a new position in Hong Kong.

Acknowledgments

This book is dedicated to Mormor, my maternal grandmother Bergthora Jonsgård, nee Kulseng, who lived all her life in Harstad in the north of Norway. She hand embroidered and I have a wonderful collection of linen stitched by her. Although she was not around to teach me to sew, I remember as a small child watching her, and I am sure she would be proud that one of her grandchildren inherited her interest in sewing.

Thank you to Jackie, Sylvia, Teresa, Carole and Georgie who helped make samples for this book and Pippa and Janette who quilted.

First published by
Quilters Haven Publications in 2014

Copyright © Karin Hellaby 2014

Graphics by Rosemary Muntus
Layout by Allan Scott & Rosemary Muntus

Photography by Kevin Mead, Art Van Go

ISBN 978-09540928-9-4
Quilters Haven Publications
68 High Street, Wickham Market
Suffolk IP13 0QU, UK

Tel: +44 (0)1728 746275
Fax: +44 (0)1728 746314

www.quilters-haven.co.uk
www.karinhellaby.com
www.quiltershavenpublications.com

Hexagons and the Bishop's Mitre

Hexagons have enjoyed a revival in recent years, and I have watched with interest as a new generation of quilters enjoy English paper piecing.

Hexi-flowers use the hexagon shape and surround it with another traditional shape known as the 'bishop's mitre'. I see the mitre as petals surrounding the centre hexagon — hence the name of this book.

All my Sew Simple books explain the quickest and most efficient techniques for patchwork, and this book is no exception. Forget having to draw templates one at a time, I have a speedier method. Forget pinning the template to the fabric, I use freezer paper and iron it in place. Forget having to cut the fabric using scissors, I use a rotary cutter, cutting several shapes at once.

Explore this book to find more methods which bring the ancient craft of sewing over papers into the 21st century.

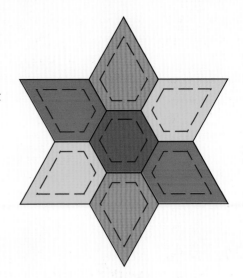

Tools and fabrics

Rotary cutting set: a small mat, rotary cutter, ruler and an add ⅜ths ruler, rotating mat.

Freezer paper: manufactured in the USA and can be purchased from quilt shops.

Propelling pencil for accurate template tracing.

Blu-Tack® to hold the paper onto the page when tracing.

Clover wonder clips to hold the paper pieces together when stitching.

Pins: silk pins for pinning when appliquéing.

Clover black gold needles for fine hand sewing.

Thimble.

Tacking or basting thread.

Bottomline thread: 100% polyester and fine enough for almost invisible stitches.

Small sharp scissors which cut right to the point.

Fabric: I have used 100% cotton patchwork fabrics. Silk fabrics would also work well.

Sewing machine is required if you are going to create shapes from two different fabrics.

Iron, Stapler.

English Paper Piecing

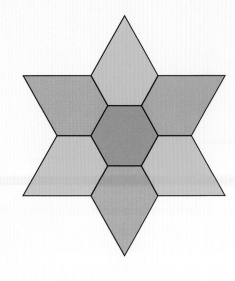

Traditional English patchwork has always been worked over papers. It is an accurate and very portable method of piecing patchwork. First the paper shapes are cut out, then the fabric is cut and tacked over the paper, and finally the patches are oversewn together by hand.

In recent years quilters have rediscovered hexagons. You can purchase ready-cut paper shapes, which are fine for this simple patchwork. But in order to make hexi-flowers it is easier to use freezer paper. This has the advantage of adhering to the fabric, eliminating the need to mark and pin fabric. I like to cut multiple templates in one go to reduce tedious marking (and, sometimes, inaccurate cutting).

1   Cut a strip of freezer paper the width of the template shape, adding 1" for ease. At one end of the strip trace the paper shape on the matt side of the freezer paper. Blu-Tack® can be used to fix the freezer paper, to prevent any movement when tracing.

2   Use a small ruler when tracing lines, as they need to be straight. A rotating pencil helps with accuracy when tracing, as you can angle the lead alongside the ruler. Continue the lines just past the template corners so that they cross. The cross marks the exact corner, making cutting out more accurate.

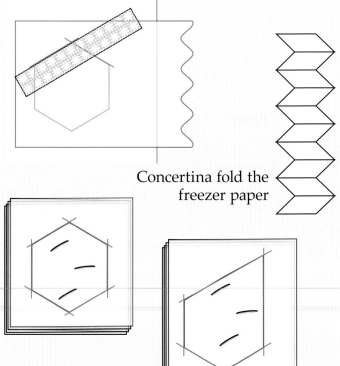

Concertina fold the freezer paper

3   Now concertina fold the freezer paper behind the drawn shape. Staple the layers together, using 2–3 staples inside the traced shape. Cut out the shape, remove the staples and you are ready to go with lots of paper shapes. The good news is that these freezer paper templates can each be used several times!

4   Iron the shiny side of the shapes to the wrong side of the fabric, leaving enough space between each shape for a ⅜" seam allowance. This allowance is easier to fold over the paper shapes and was traditionally used in this technique. There is no need to measure the seam allowance (it can be eyeballed!) but when I like to be neat with even seam allowances I use an add ⅜" ruler. This allows me to rotary cut the fabric. A rotating mat is useful at this stage.

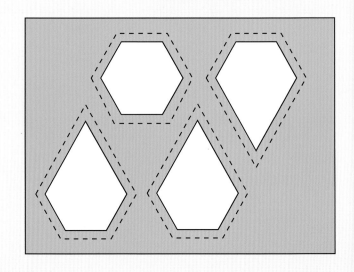

QH Tip

For multiple fabric shapes, cut squares of fabric larger than the template plus seam allowance.

Layer four to six, ironing a template to the top fabric. Carefully rotary cut, adding seam allowance to template by using the add ⅜" ruler.

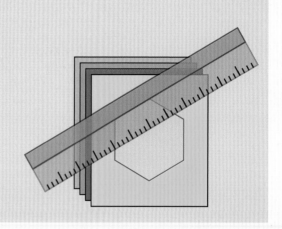

5 Fold the fabric allowance over the paper and tack down with a neutral-coloured thread. Beware of cheap coloured sewing threads, as they can bleed into your fabric.

Start with the knot on the right side as it will be easier to remove later. You will only need to tack two or three stitches on each side of the shape. As a right-hander work anti-clockwise from the wrong side, so it will be easier to appliqué the points later. Make neat corners by taking a stitch over each fold. Always ensure the fabric is tightly folded over the paper.

Where you have sharp points to tack down, do not tuck in the point – simply leave it free, as the tails will be hidden under the appliqué when sewn onto the background fabric.

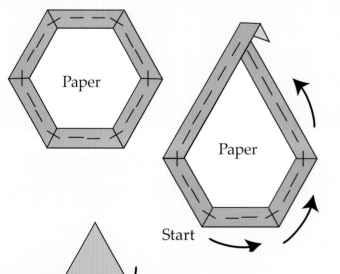

6 Once you have tacked enough shapes you can lay out your design and then start to sew the pieces together.

Use a good quality fine cotton thread or (my preference) Bottomline polyester thread, and knot one end. I use a fine needle to sew the small stitches.

7 With right sides of shapes together, use an overstitch (whip stitch) to join the patches. Use a thread that closely matches at least one of your fabrics.

5

8 I use a wonder clip to hold the two shapes together without pinning.

Start sewing about ¼" from a corner, work two or three overstitches into the corner, then oversew to the next corner, crossing over the starting stitches. Pick up another patch and continue oversewing.

You finish off by oversewing two stitches back from the corner, again crossing over the previous stitches and finishing off.

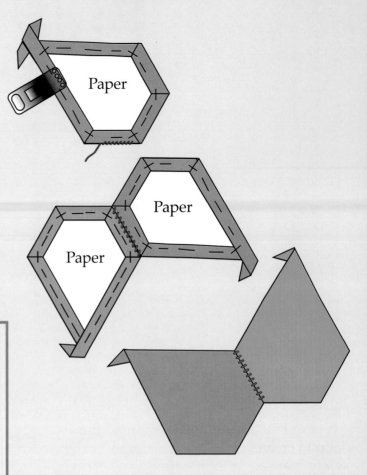

Paper

Paper

Paper

Using the right sized templates

I have given you four different sizes for both templates; 1" is the smallest and 2.5" is the largest. The hexagon side fits the shortest side of the equivalent bishop's mitre.

Templates	Flower size
1"	7"
1.5"	10.5"
2"	14"
2.5"	17.5"

How to thread a needle

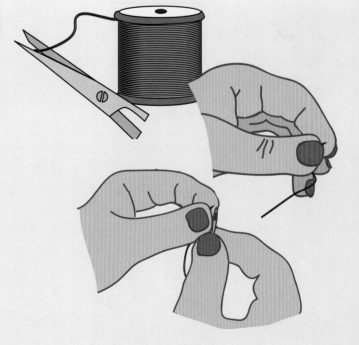

The needle should be threaded with the end of the thread that is coming off the reel. Using sharp scissors, cut this at an angle to create a point on the thread end. At this stage do not cut the thread off the reel.

Pinch the pointed end between the thumb and forefinger of your left hand, only allowing a tiny length of thread to show. Suck the eye of the needle – the saliva will attract the thread. Take the eye of the needle to the thread. Once threaded, cut a length of approximately 18" from the reel.

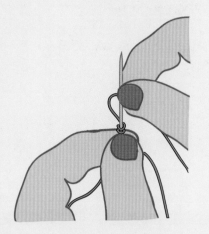

How to tie a Quilter's knot

Hold the threaded needle in your left hand, pinching it halfway, between your thumb and forefinger. The needle should be pointing upwards. Wrap the thread around the needle two or three times. Pull the needle upwards, while continuing to pinch the wrapped thread. Continue pinching and pulling until you form a small knot at the end of the thread. Pull the knot tight.

Finishing with a securing stitch

Finish with a securing stitch to prevent your stitching from coming undone. At the back of the work, take one small backstitch through the back of the work *only* and make a loop over the point of the needle. Pull the thread through the loop to create a knot at the base of the fabric. For a stronger secure stitch, repeat the process to create two knots.

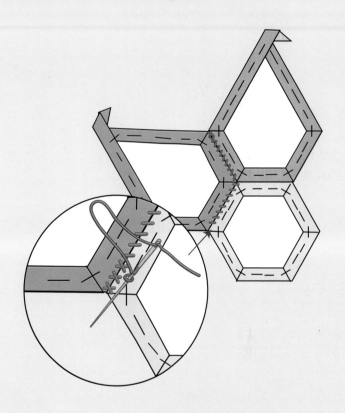

Finishing with a textile knot

Alternatively take a backstitch through the back of the fabric only. Place the needle as if you were going to make another backstitch, but do not pull the needle through.

You have a single thread at the front. Place it under the needle from left to right. Take the two threads at the back and bring them forward, placing them under the needle from right to left. Place your thumb on the needle as you pull the thread through. You will have a knot on the back surface of your work. Now hide the end of the thread by stitching it back into the fabric.

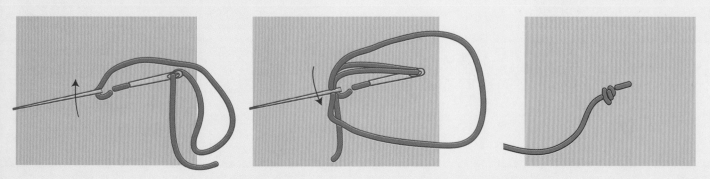

Top left: Meandering in the Meadow *(41″ × 75″) made and quilted by Jackie Nekrews*

Top right: Bouquet *(30″ × 42″) made and quilted by Teresa Wardlaw*

Left: Mini iPad Cover *(8¾″ × 13″) made using 1″ templates and quilted by Karin Hellaby*

Right: Jester *(21″ × 21″) made using 1″ templates and quilted by Carole Redman*

This page has been left
blank intentionally.

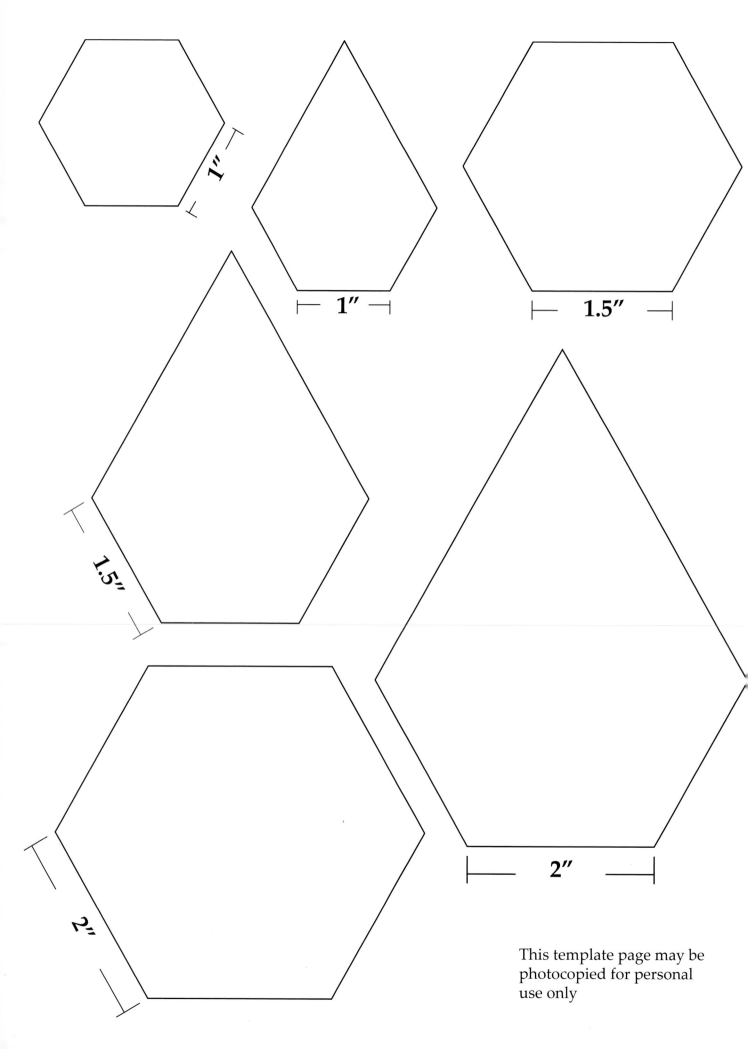

1"

1"

1.5"

1.5"

2"

2"

This template page may be
photocopied for personal
use only

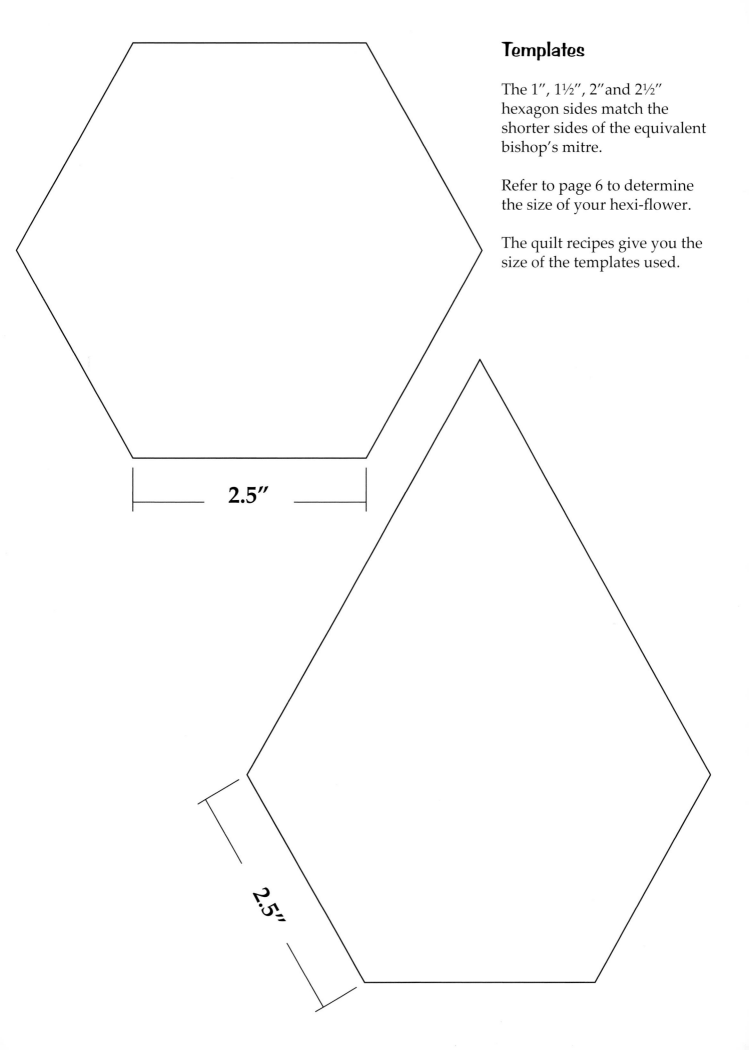

Templates

The 1″, 1½″, 2″ and 2½″ hexagon sides match the shorter sides of the equivalent bishop's mitre.

Refer to page 6 to determine the size of your hexi-flower.

The quilt recipes give you the size of the templates used.

2.5″

2.5″

This page has been left
blank intentionally.

Above: Fantasy Flowers *(15″ × 18″) made using 1″ templates and quilted by Karin Hellaby*

Top left: Serenade The Flowers *(42″ × 55″) made and quilted by Georgina Smith*

Below: Moonflower Garden *(40″ × 42″) made using 2″ templates by Karin Hellaby, quilted by Janette Chilver*

Right: Shimmer Table Runner *(15″ × 43½″) made using 1″ templates and quilted by Karin Hellaby*

Below: Shimmer Pillow *(18″ × 18″) made and quilted by Karin Hellaby*

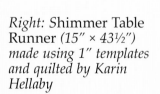

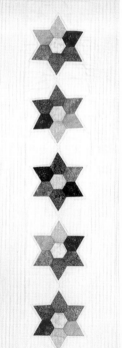

9

Sewing hexi-flowers to a background

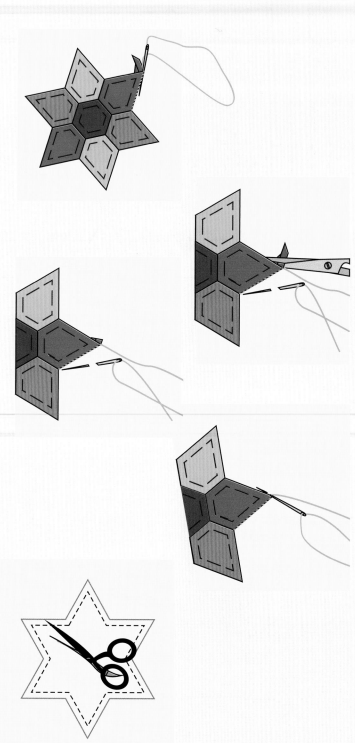

I leave the papers inside my work until after I have sewn it to the background. This gives me a firm edge to appliqué.

1 Pin the patchwork onto the background, making sure you are keeping within the seam allowances. I then move the pins to the wrong side so that my thread does not catch on the pins

2 Use an invisible hand appliqué stitch. Start stitching halfway along one side, with a knot placed on the back, and pull the needle through the folded fabric edge.

Directly opposite where the needle has emerged, go straight down into the background fabric *only* and come back through the seam allowance fold, ⅛" away from the first stitch. Repeat, taking one stitch at a time.

Stitches on the right side should be straight and almost invisible. On the back of your work the stitches will look slanted as the stitch travels the ⅛".

Stitch to the point, then take one stitch back and another back to the point to fix the point. Trim the excess fabric to less than ¼", and snip the tacking thread to allow you to fold the excess fabric under the template

3 When you have finished the appliqué, remove the pins and cut the background fabric away from the back, cutting ⅜" inside the stitching line.

4 Remove the papers from the back and reuse them, unless the edges are torn.

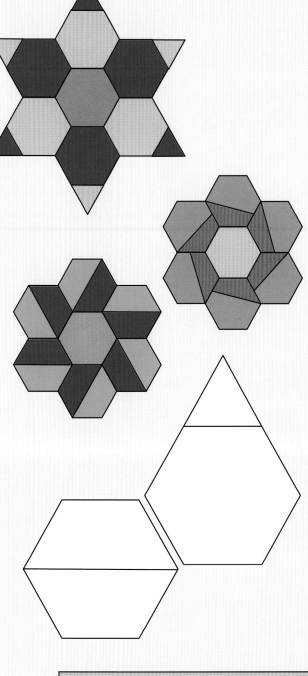

Drawing a new line inside the template shapes will lead you into lots of new and exciting patchwork

Dividing the templates with an additional line does not increase the amount of hand sewing.

1 Draw a new line on the matt side of the freezer paper. I like to draw this from one corner to the opposite corner, or to the middle of a side. Suggestions can be seen on the inside front cover.

2 Next cut the fabric strips. To calculate the width of the fabric strips, measure the template from the pencilled line to the furthest point on the template and add 1", for seam allowances.

Repeat for the second strip measurement.

Sew these two strips by machine, using a ¼" seam allowance, and press the seam open.

3 Position the freezer paper template shiny side down, with the new pencilled line on the open seam. Iron in place.

Then cut out and proceed as before.

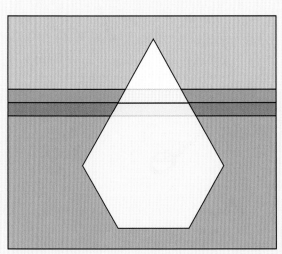

Quilt recipes

Shimmer 45" × 58"

- Approximately 50 × 5" charm squares
- 1¾ yards background grey fabric
- Uses the 1" hexagon and 1" bishop's mitre templates.

Cut two bishop's mitre shapes from each charm square. Cut two to four hexagons from one charm square. Follow instructions to make 14 hexi-flowers.

Cut the background fabric to the quilt size. Appliqué the flowers onto the background. Layer, quilt and bind.

Right: Shimmer detail, made and quilted by Karin Hellaby. For full quilt see the title page.

Below: Fresh Flower Garden (36" × 36") made and quilted by Karin Hellaby

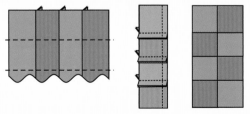

More recipes...

You'll find more recipes on our website at www.quilters-haven.co.uk – and please do send us *your* pictures for the web gallery!

Fresh Flower Garden 36" × 36"

- ½ yard white, cut into 8 × 8½" background squares
- ½ yard blue, cut six 2½" strips; four will be used in the border
- ¼ yard green, cut two 2½" strips
- ½ yard stripe for binding

Use the 1" hexagon and bishop's mitre templates to make the hexi-flowers. The new template line on the mitre is drawn from the outside corner to half way down the opposite side. Make sure these are all drawn the same. Follow the instructions on page 11 and then make up the hexi-flowers following the instructions on page 5.

Appliqué one flower onto the centre of a background square.

Make two strip sets with alternating 2½" strips in blue, green, blue, green (four strips in each set). Press all seams in one direction. Straighten one end of the strip set.

Cut 32 2½" pieces: each piece will have four fabric squares in a strip. Stitch four pieces together to make a 16-square block. Press; each block should measure 8½". Stitch the blocks together as seen in the quilt. Add 2½" borders. Layer, quilt and bind with striped fabric.

Lollipop Flowers 47" × 49"

- ⅛ yard cuts from 15 fabrics for hexi-flowers
- ¼ yard yellow for flowers and cornerstones
- ¼ yard from two greens for stems and leaves
- ½ yard border
- ½ yard binding
- 1¼ yards white background. Cut 38" × 41" piece

Use the 1½" bishop's mitre and hexagon templates to make the eight flowers. The new line is drawn 2" from the base of the mitre. A 1" hexagon has also been used for some of the flower centres. Once the flowers are made, appliqué to the white background, leaving a small open space to insert the stem.

Above right: Lollipop Flowers *detail (for the complete quilt see front cover)*

Left: Clockwise Table Runner (14" × 45") made and quilted by Teresa Wardlaw

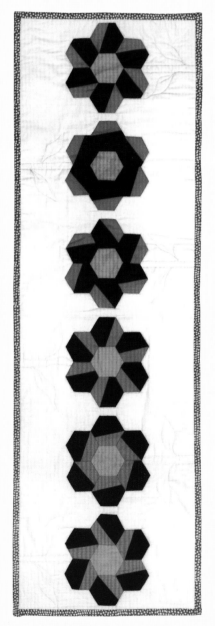

Stems

Cut 1" × 7" lengths. Fold under ¼" on the long sides. Appliqué in place.

Leaves

These are made using the 1" bishop's mitre and appliquéd at the side of the stems.

Border

Cut four 5" wide border strips, width of fabric. Cut four 5" cornerstones. Add to the sides of the quilt. Layer, quilt and bind.

Clockwise Table Runner 11" × 35"

- 11" × 35" background fabric, can be pieced.
- ½ yard of two plain fabrics for flower outside hexagons
- ⅛ yard centre hexagons
- ¼ yard binding

This is a variation of the traditional grandmother's flower garden, with a centre hexagon surrounded by six pieced hexagons. By rotating clockwise where the seam occurs on the outer hexagons, different flowers appear. Use the 1" hexagon template to make the hexi-flowers. Each flower uses templates with the same line and colour combination.

Cut and stitch two fabric strips, following the instructions on page 11. Appliqué the six grandmother hexi-flowers to the background fabric. Layer, quilt and bind.

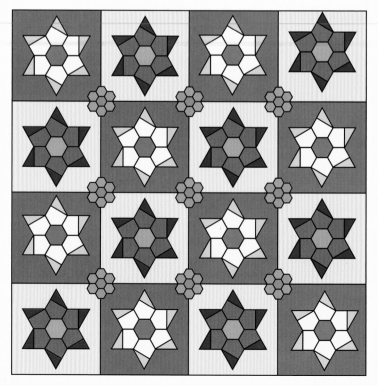

Ideas for quilts, coverlets, runners and cushions

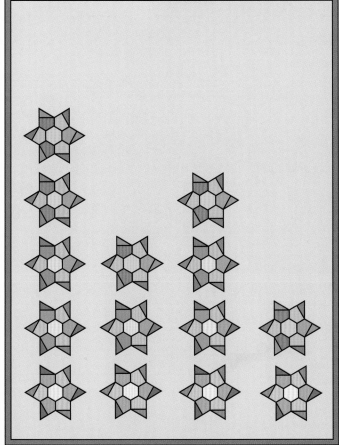

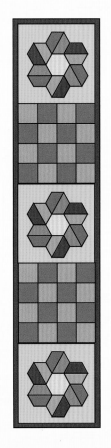

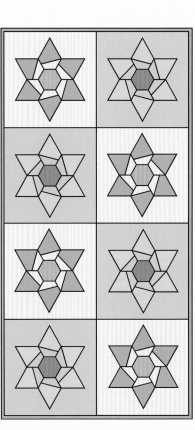

Finishing

Nearly all these quilts have hexi-flowers applied to a single piece of fabric cut to the size of the final quilt. This makes quilting and finishing them so simple. But if you want to mix the flowers with blocks, and/or add a border as in *Fresh Flower Garden* on page 12, assemble and press well.

Cut or piece your backing 3" larger than the finished quilt and cut your wadding (batting) just a little smaller. Secure the backing (wrong side up) on a flat surface with tape, place the wadding on top and finally your quilt top, right side up. Keep the layers together with safety pins or basting spray. Machine or hand quilt, and then trim off the excess wadding and backing fabric. Baste the outer edge of the quilt ¼" inside the quilt edge, to keep edges together, and then bind.

I love to use a striped fabric for bindings – it looks so effective! Of course the technique described can be used with any cotton fabrics.

Cut enough 2¾" wide fabric strips to go all the way around the quilt, with an excess of 24". Join the binding strips at short ends with a straight seam. Press seams open. Fold the binding strip in half, wrong sides together. Press.

Use a ⅜" seam allowance and a walking foot when stitching the binding to the front of the quilt. Start at the bottom of the quilt, halfway along, leaving a tail of 9".

Stop sewing ⅜" from the next corner, turn slightly and stitch diagonally to the outside corner. Lift the presser foot and turn the quilt. Fold the binding up and then down so that the fold is even with the quilt edge. Pin. Stitch down to the next corner, and repeat for all four corners.

Finish stitching approximately 10" from the start point. Lay the end of the binding within the fold of the start binding. Lay flat. Mark the overlap with a line. Remove from fold and cut any excess binding fabric ½" away from the marked line. Pin the ends of the binding together, matching raw edges, and join with a ¼" seam. Press this seam open. Fold back in half and stitch into place.

Depending on the wadding used, either iron or finger press the binding away from the front. Fold to the back of the quilt and hand sew into place.

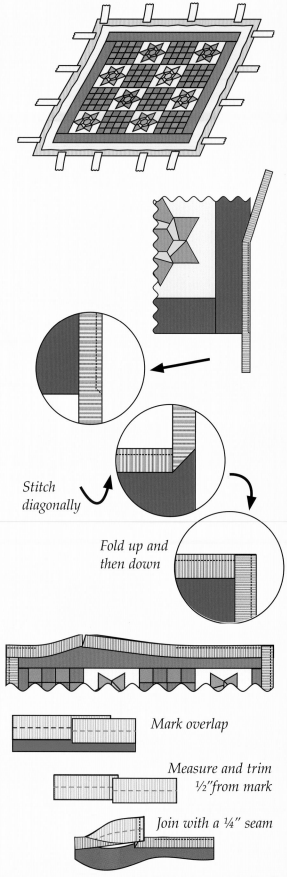

Stitch diagonally

Fold up and then down

Mark overlap

Measure and trim ½"from mark

Join with a ¼" seam